MIKE CARPENTER

ATHENS

*Its History, Its Art,
Its Landmarks*

CONTENTS

History   3

The old Acropolis   21

The Parthenon   27

The later Acropolis   31

The Areopagus   37

The Agora   41

The Temple of Hephaestus   47

The Roman Agora   51

The Arch of Hadrian   55

The Temple of Olympian Zeus   59

The Panathenaic Stadium   61

The Roman Baths at Zappeion   67

The Academy   69

Syntagma Square   73

Monastiraki Square   77

The Plaka   81

Lycabettus Hill   83

Museums   85

HISTORY

A s so often happens with very old cities, Athens' origins are rooted in myth. And, since we are talking about Ancient Greece, several gods and goddesses are involved. The story goes that the god Hephaestus wanted to make out with the virgin goddess Athena, who had no intention of going along. Athena was an offspring of Zeus, king of the gods on Mount Olympus, and his first wife, the goddess Metis, daughter of Titans Oceanus and Tethys. Athena managed to escape Hephaestus's heavy-handed advances, but the god was already aroused enough to leave an unwelcome souvenir on Athena's leg in the form of a residue of his semen. Disgusted, Athena cleaned that trace of Hephaestus's lust and threw away the cloth she had used. Yet, since divine seed could never be wasted, it fertilized the goddess Gaia, the personification of the Earth.

That impromptu insemination resulted in

Erichthonius, who would later become Athens' fourth legendary king. This myth encouraged the Athenians to consider themselves a special lot. As famed playwright Euripides – one of the three greats of Greek dramaturgy, together with Aeschylus and Sophocles – wrote in 431 BCE in his tragedy titled *Medea*, Athenians are happy because they are "children of the blessed gods, born from an uncontaminated land." Thus, Athens' citizens were not only *autochthonous*, which in Greek means "of their own land" and, by extension, indigenous, but also of divine origin.

Upon those origins, Ancient Athenians have always founded their feeling of superiority toward everybody else and the rigid organization of their society. Athens' citizens were all equal among themselves but, simultaneously, very different from and superior to anyone from foreign lands. It is no coincidence that they called all foreigners not fluent in the Greek language *bárbaros*, an onomatopoeic word that means stutterers. If you couldn't speak and write Greek, you were considered a savage, if not a disabled person. That's also why Athenian democracy, though widely praised as a beacon of light at a time when examples of such kind of government were few and far between, only encompassed between 10% and 20% of the adult population. Among those not allowed to take part in the city's political life were all women, obviously the enslaved people, estimated at 30% to 40% of the population or more, and all foreigners residing in the town permanently, the so-called metics, freemen who weren't counted among Athens' citizens.

Metics (from a Greek word meaning "alien" or "temporary") had many duties, complemented by a handful of rights, and were an essential part of Athenian society. Most were artisans, and some industries, such as pottery, were in their hands. The poorest ones had menial jobs, such as hustlers, dealers, or even snitches. Women were often employed as nannies, courtesans, or flutists. A minority of metics were people of means, so much so as to have an important role in Athens' economy as grain importers, shipowners, or even bankers. Some were doctors, architects, or *logográfoi*, i.e., writers of judicial speeches. They had to pay taxes and were required to serve in the military, primarily in the all-important Navy. Despite this, they were not allowed to marry an Athenian citizen or to own land unless through a special decree. They could not be elected judges or ministers, but unlike other foreigners, they could act in a lawsuit and speak publicly.

The symbol of Athens is the Owl of Athena, the goddess that gave the city its name [see drawing on page 1]. Its origins are unclear, but the owl is believed to represent wisdom and knowledge, a perfect complement to Athena, the goddess of wisdom and warfare, and Athens, the cradle of philosophy. On the owl's right, the letters AOE stand for the word AΘHNAIΩN, which can be translated as "of the Athenians." On the owl's left, an olive branch refers back to the goddess, who gifted the precious olive tree to the Athenians, while a crescent – a quarter moon that, in heraldry, is a symbol of nobility – adds solemnity to the whole scene. Owl images were used on vases, plates, amphorae, and other artifacts. The complete symbolic image can be found on coins and bas-reliefs dating back as far as 510 BCE. Even to this day, Greece's one-euro coin depicts the exact same motif used two and a half millennia ago.

Athens' founding hero was Theseus, whose myth is worth telling. As the story goes, for a while, Athens was a tributary of Crete, a competing Greek city-state. At that time, Crete's ruler was the mighty king Minos, whose parents were believed to be the god Zeus and the mortal Europa. Minos also wrote Crete's constitution, allegedly with the help of his powerful father. After Minos's only son, Androgeus, was killed in battle against Athens, he demanded a tribute of fifteen Athenian boys and fifteen girls to be sent to him every nine years (other sources speak of seven guys and seven girls every year). They were meant to feed the monstrous Minotaur, a being with human features but a bull's head resulting from a prior deception by Crete's king toward the god Poseidon, one of the Twelve Olympians, as an expiatory sacrifice.

This practice continued until Theseus, son of Athens' king Aegeus, took it upon himself to put an end to this horrible practice. Shipped to Crete with that year's group of sacrificial victims, he killed the Minotaur and escaped from the Labyrinth of Knossos, where the flesh-eating beast was held captive, thanks to the help of Minos's daughter Ariadne and her famous thread. On his way home, Theseus showed a certain degree of ungratefulness toward

Ariadne, leaving her behind on the island of Naxos after falling in love with her younger sister, Phaedra. The cold hand of fate, though, had a bad ending in store for Theseus: he forgot to hoist the white sails in place of the black ones, as agreed with his father before leaving Athens, inducing his august parent to take his life by throwing himself into the sea. Hence, the name of the sea lapping at Greece's coast, the Aegean Sea, was born.

* * *

Moving on from myth to history, it is thought that Athens was founded around 1500 BCE in the area of the Acropolis Hill by an Ionian populace. For many centuries, it was a center of minor importance, overshadowed by cities like Argos, Mycenae, and Tirino. Initially a monarchy, the king's power slowly waned over time. A warrior aristocracy (the *eupatridae*) was able to gradually take over control, reducing the sovereign's role. From the tenth to the seventh century BCE, the governing power rested with a group of six to nine *archons*, magistrates chosen exclusively from the ranks of Athens' aristocracy.

Athens' great breakthrough started in the seventh century BCE, when written laws progressively replaced the earlier customary law. The first legislator who made history was Draco. Taking advantage of the constant infighting between the archons, Draco took control of the city-state and gave it a set of laws harsh enough to be remembered to this day in the expression of *draconian laws* (or *draconian punishments)*. Using his full powers, Draco enacted his Code (also called the Draconian Constitution) in 621 BCE. Perhaps the most consequential of the new rules was Draco's decision to ban honor killings. In Ancient Athens, violently avenging the wrongs suffered was central to one's ability to keep social standing. Homer's poems describe several prime examples of this mindset, which was an inescapable necessity for anyone looking to be respected by their peers. Draco understood that Athens' civic progress was hindered by such an ill-advised custom that caused permanent belligerence between family clans, and he outlawed honor killings. From that moment on, every homicide would be treated in the same way. Draco's body of legislation, Athens' first written one, is considered by many a first step toward what would become Athenian democracy.

Draco was followed by a succession of reformers who, over a couple of centuries, strengthened and perfected Athens' democratic institutions, making this ancient city-state an example of a democratic regime at a time when absolute rule by a king, tyrant, or small oligarchy was the most common form of government in the world by far. First among them was Solon, an enlightened aristocrat appointed to archon in 594 BCE. His interventions were mostly in the fields of economic relationships between citizens and the judiciary. Under his authority, debt bondage was banned. Before Solon's reforms, many peasants were enslaved to all intents and purposes due to Athens' unreasonable rules about the distribution of the harvest between them, who only took home one-sixth of the yield, and the aristocracy of landowners, who were entitled to the rest. Thus, it was common for farmers to end up in debt and ultimately in a state of serfdom. Under Solon, they regained their freedom.

Another innovation Solon introduced was rearranging the citizenry into four classes based on wealth. This allowed for more open access to public office. Besides the aristocracy of blood, the aristocracy of money could now hold the highest political and administrative offices. The two lowest (poorest) classes, *zeugitae* and *thetes*, were involved in civic life mainly as soldiers (the *hoplites*).

Last but not least, Solon established the *Heliaia*, a sort of supreme court on which all male citizens of Athens over the age of thirty were eligible to serve. This highest court inherited from the *Areopagus* and the archons the responsibility of judging crimes and civil cases. It consisted of six thousand members chosen annually by lot and divided into chambers of six hundred members each. Each of Athens' ten tribes contributed to the court with six hundred members, ensuring its democratic composition. For the first time ever, one could expect to be judged by a jury of fellow citizens (a jury of peers, so to speak, as later sanctioned in England's *Magna Charta* in 1215 CE).

Interestingly, the Solonian constitution was written as poetry, not prose, reflecting Ancient Greeks' huge respect for the noble art. Furthermore, as soon as his code of laws was introduced, Solon went into a ten-year self-imposed exile. With all his accumulated prestige and power, he could have easily become Athens' tyrant. As a ruler motivated by true democratic sentiments, that was a temptation he wanted to avoid at all costs.

Not all of Solon's reforms were crowned by lasting success, which led to several periods of tyranny in Athens between 561 and 510 BCE, first under Pisistratus, then under his son Hippias. It was Cleisthenes, a member of the powerful aristocratic Alcmaeonid family, to end that dark time in Athens' history. After rising to power in 508 BCE, Cleisthenes divided the territory of Attica – the Greek peninsula where Athens is located – into one hundred *demi*, administrative units comprising the population without class distinction or privileges. Every demo had its own assembly and leader – the *demarchos* – who had the power to rule autonomously about matters concerning the demo itself.

Furthermore, Cleisthenes instituted ten tribes – the *phylai* – and a legislative body called *Boule*, whose five hundred members were chosen by lot. Each of the ten tribes was entitled to fifty seats, and each oversaw the government of the city-state for one-tenth of the year, giving every part of Athens' citizenry the feeling of shared responsibility. As not all periods of the year were equally important, the order in which each tribe led the assembly was also randomly selected yearly.

The Boule was the body that decided which political matters and legislative initiatives were worthy of a debate before the Areopagus council, Athens' highest court traditionally reserved for its aristocratic families. As a whole, Cleisthenes's reforms reduced the aristocracy's influence over political decisions and produced a more decentralized and democratic form of government.

Perhaps the most illustrious and prominent of all Athenian legislators was Pericles. Elected to the office of *strategos* (military commander) in 460 BCE, in the first of fifteen such appointments, he went on to dominate the following thirty years of Athens' public life. Building on the foundation left by his predecessors, he strengthened the city's democratic structures enough to become almost synonymous with it.

If we believe Thucydides – the famed Ancient Greece historian – Pericles's power and long career rested on his reputation, political cleverness, indisputable incorruptibility, and ability to rule over his fellow citizens without limiting their freedom. The trust and respect he had earned from the city-state's people allowed him to make fifth-century BCE Athens the universal model of democratic governance that was later followed almost everywhere. He was much more than a mere, if exceptionally gifted, statesman. He loved art and culture and was friends with the sculptor Phidias, the tragedian Sophocles, the historian Herodotus, and the philosopher Anaxagoras.

Under Pericles's leadership, the archonship was rendered accessible to all citizen classes created by Solon's reform except the last, poorest one. A large portion of the population felt included in the city-state's political life at the highest level for the first time. His second innovation was groundbreaking: he granted every citizen participating in the Heliaia and the Boule a stipend (the *misthos*), a measure destined to make it easier for citizens of limited means to participate in Athens' public life. Pericles destined funds coming from the taxation of Athens' allies in the Delian League to the financing of his reform, meaning that the city's democratic development was subsidized by its imperialism, as some critics argue. The misthos was abolished toward the end of the century, after Pericles's death.

Pericles's famous Funeral Oration for the first Athenian soldiers killed in the Peloponnesian War fought against Sparta and the Peloponnesian League, as handed down by Thucydides, remains forever engrained in history:

Our form of government does not enter into rivalry with the institutions of others. Our government does not copy our neighbors', but is an example to them. It is true that we are called a democracy, for the administration is in the hands of the many and not of the few. But while there exists equal justice to all and alike in their private disputes, the claim of excellence is also recognized; and when a citizen is in any way distinguished, he is preferred to the public service, not as a matter of privilege, but as the reward of merit. Neither is poverty an obstacle, but a man may benefit his country whatever the obscurity of his condition. [From Pericles's Funeral Oration, 430 BCE]

To wrap up this brief summary of Athens'

democratic development, it needs to be noted that Greek democracy always remained the privilege of the few – i.e., male citizens with full political rights – while enslavement, essential to the economic success of so many ancient societies, was the natural plight of the many. It is believed that up to one in two Ancient Athens inhabitants were enslaved, depending on the historical period.

Of course, besides being the "cradle of democracy", Athens also was where philosophy flourished to the point of becoming the bedrock of Western rational thinking. Greek philosophy would go on to influence Western thinkers for ages, including Christian ones. But this part of Greece had no role in developing philosophical thought until Anaxagoras, born in Clazomenae – in Asia Minor – in 496 BCE, relocated to Pericles's Athens in 462 BCE. Later came Socrates (470-399 BCE), widely considered the father of Western ethics, followed by his disciple Plato (428-348 BCE), who, in turn, had Aristotle (384-322 BCE) among his pupils. Besides leaving an enormous body of work that profoundly influenced Western philosophy for centuries, Aristotle also was a teacher to Alexander the Great (356-323 BCE), the man who created an empire spanning from Macedonia and the Adriatic Sea to the Indus River in faraway India, encompassing modern-day Turkey, Syria, Jordan, Israel, Egypt, Iraq, Iran, Afghanistan, and Pakistan.

* * *

The traditional and most menacing rival of Greece's city-states has always been the Persian Empire, founded in 550 BCE by Cyrus II of Persia. At its highest expansion, this empire stretched from the northern shores of Africa to the borders of India, encompassing the entire Middle East and modern-day Turkey. It is believed that Emperor Darius I of the Achaemenid dynasty ruled over half of the world's population in his heyday, at the beginning of the fifth century BCE.

The first big showdown between Athens and the Persian Empire came in 490 BCE. When, in 499 BCE, a group of Greek cities located on modern-day Turkey's western coast had rebelled against the empire under the leadership of Miletus, a vibrant coastal town with a lively intellectual, economic, and political life, Darius had destroyed the city, enslaved its inhabitants, and deported them to Mesopotamia. After subduing the other rebellious towns in Asia Minor, too, he focused on Athens, which had had the audacity to support Miletus's revolt with a small contingent of twenty warships. In 490 BCE, he sent twenty-five thousand men and six hundred ships to teach a lesson to those brazen Greeks. He was in for a rude awakening. Led by the strategos Miltiades, ten thousand Greek hoplites decisively defeated the Persian expeditionary force at the Battle of Marathon, losing only two hundred men. For now, Athens was safe.

The Persians were not going to accept such a humiliating defeat without responding in kind. In 480 BCE, after ten years of preparation, Darius's son

Xerxes I felt ready to strike again. This time, the Persian army consisted of no less than one hundred thousand men supported by a navy of at least six hundred ships. Xerxes sent this gigantic expedition force to conquer all of Greece, but things did not go as planned. This time, Greece's city-states, including the powerful Sparta, had joined forces against the common foe. The Persian army was initially held up for seven days at the mountain pass of Thermopylae, where just three hundred Spartans led by their king Leonidas I and aided by a couple thousand men from the allies sacrificed themselves to the last man in an unequal fight to slow down Xerxes's troops (as recounted, with some artistic license, in the 2006 movie *300*, by director Zack Snyder). After overcoming Leonidas's resistance, the Persian army swiftly occupied most of Attica. Athens was captured and sacked, but the war was far from over.

The Persian army could not reach Sparta, located farther south on the Peloponnese peninsula, separated from Attica by the narrow and easily defensible Isthmus of Corinth. Meanwhile, the powerful Athenian fleet, led by Themistocles and the Spartan Eurybiades, decisively defeated the Persian one at the Battle of Salamis, fought in the straits between the mainland and the island of Salamis, just offshore from Athens. This battle, fought on 23 September 480 BCE, marked the end of the Persians' hopes to subjugate the Greeks. Now deprived of their fleet's support, about one year later the Persian army was defeated by the Greek alliance led by the Spartan general Pausanias, a nephew of Leonidas I, at the

Battle of Plataea, a city in the region of Boeotia northwest of Athens. The final blow to Xerxes's invasion came shortly after at the Battle of Mycale, where the Persian army's and fleet's remains were destroyed.

The alliance of the Greek city-states had won and, with it, the Greek civilization. Some historians even believe that, had the Persians conquered the Greeks, Pericles's Athens would never have flourished. The history of Western civilization might have been different from how we know it.

Still, the alliance between Athens and Sparta was a marriage of convenience, destined to end sooner rather than later. War broke out in 431 BCE and lasted until 404 BCE, when the Peloponnesian League led by Sparta achieved victory against the Delian League led by Athens. The Peloponnesian War changed the face of Ancient Greece forever. Athens would never regain its prominence and prosperity. When the clash with Sparta was over, Athens' power was severely reduced, and much of Greece, battered by a long period of destruction that had claimed countless lives, saw a strong economic decline. Thus, the Peloponnesian War is considered by many the closing act of the Hellenic civilization's golden century.

Our main source of knowledge about this conflict is the *History of the Peloponnesian War* by famed Athenian historian and general Thucydides, which tells the events up to 411 BCE. In Thucydides' view, a war between Athens and Sparta had become inevitable because of the rise of Athens and the fear that this instilled in Sparta. This concept became later known as the "Thucydides Trap," whereby when a rising superpower – e.g., Athens – challenges the dominance of an established one – e.g., Sparta – they are "destined for war" (see the eponymous book by author Graham T. Allison, where the U.S. takes the role of Sparta and modern-day China stands for Ancient Athens).

After its defeat against Sparta, Athens was never again able to rise to its ancient prominence. In 338 BCE, Athens lost its autonomy as a city-state at the hands of the Macedonian king Philip II, Alexander the Great's father. In 337 BCE, Philip formed the Corinthian League, an alliance that replaced all previous leagues between Greek *poleis* (city-states) and included almost all Greek cities except for Sparta. All participants acknowledged Macedonia's supremacy and promised they would not go to war against each other.

Later on, it was unavoidable for Rome, the nascent superpower that would one day dominate every corner of the Mediterranean region, to come into contact with a declining Athens. The Pyrrhic War (280-275 BCE) was the first military conflict that saw the ascending Roman power confronted by the professional mercenary armies of the Hellenistic city-states. The clash originated from Rome's aggressive expansion into the southern part of the Italian peninsula, which prompted the city of Taranto to call on Pyrrhus, king of Epirus, for assistance against the Romans. Taranto was part of Magna Graecia, a string of Hellenistic cities founded on Italian shores, mainly in Sicily, Apulia, and Lucania (modern-day Calabria and Basilicata), but with settlements as far north as Capua, not far from Naples.

Pyrrhus crossed the Adriatic Sea at the helm of thirty-one thousand men and some twenty elephants, including reinforcements from several allies. Pyrrhus's plan was to liberate Taranto from the Romans' siege and expand his authority into Sicily and even attack Carthage, in modern-day Tunisia, a long-standing enemy of Magna Graecia's Greek cities. After initial successes at the battles of Heraclea (280 BCE) and Asculum in Apulia (279 BCE), Pyrrhus's fleet was comprehensively defeated by the Carthaginians in the Battle of the Strait of Messina, between Sicily and the Italian peninsula, where Pyrrhus lost a big part of his army (276 BCE).

Once again confronted by the Roman troops, Pyrrhus suffered the decisive defeat of his Italian campaign at the Battle of Maleventum in modern-day Campania (275 BCE), after which he had to retreat back to Greece, where he died in battle against the combined forces of Macedonia and Sparta in 272 BCE. Ironically, it was Rome, more than a century later, to conquer, plunder, and completely destroy Carthage, Pyrrhus's ancient foe, at the end of the Third Punic War (146 BCE). Pyrrhus's catastrophic Italian campaign gave birth to the expression "Pyrrhic victory," meaning a victory so costly for the winners to lead to their consequent demise. His early successes in battle had proven so punishing for his army to lay the foundation for his eventual defeat.

In 146 BCE, after conquering Macedonia, the

increasingly powerful Rome – still a republic at that point – annexed the entirety of continental Greece, making it a protectorate part of the Roman province of Macedonia. After giving the world its first example of democratic rule (sort of) and laying the foundations of Western philosophy, Athens was reduced to one of many dominions of a rising Rome. In 49 CE, the apostle Paul reached Athens on his second missionary journey up and down the empire, bringing the first taste of the Christian faith to that city of proud philosophical thinkers and polemicists. He made his case in the Areopagus, where Athens' citizens were fond of discussing all matters concerning religious cults and philosophical beliefs. This is where Socrates was sentenced to death for corrupting Athens' youth and introducing new divinities (the reference was to his *daimon*). Paul fought valiantly but could not stop the Athenians from ridiculing him when he proclaimed Jesus's resurrection from the dead. Unlike Socrates, Paul could at least depart unharmed.

THE OLD ACROPOLIS

The Acropolis, a word meaning "upper city," is both a hill in the middle of the city and its religious heart. Historically, most cities in Ancient Greece were built around a central area where the sovereign resided, and which was easy to defend. Athens' Acropolis can be traced back to the Mycenaean civilization that occupied the site in the Late Bronze Age, around 1600-1100 BCE. It had the typical defense walls and a prince's palace. The later Greek civilization added a sanctuary and several temples to honor the gods.

Emerging from the extensive built-up area of Athens, which resembles a vast, restless sea of houses and streets breaking against its sides, the Acropolis looks like a big ship raising its prow above it all on its eastern side. At its highest point, the Mycenaeans had built the open-air sanctuary of Zeus Polieus, patron of the city, of which only some remnants of the foundations survive. The arrival of a new people, the Greeks, led to the destruction of the prince's palace, the Mycenaean civilization's most significant testimony. On its ruins, the new residents erected a temple to Athena, the goddess of wisdom, the arts, and military strategy, that gave her name to the city.

According to the myth, initially, Athena had to share her temple with some tombs from Athens' distant past, most importantly that of its sixth king, Erechtheus. This is also where a dispute between Athena and Poseidon, the god of the sea, earthquakes, and seaquakes, took place about the dominion over the Acropolis. The feud was resolved in Athena's favor after she gifted the city an olive tree, while Poseidon's gift was a horse. An imprint from the god's trident was said to be left on a rock.

The city walls, though, survived the destruction of the old prince's palace. They were strong enough to constitute a credible defense for this part of the city until the siege by the Persians in 480 BCE.

The first ruler to massively contribute to the Acropolis's architectural splendor was Pisistratus, a polemarch – the city's supreme military commander – who later ruled Athens as a tyrant on two occasions between 560 and 528 BCE. South of the archaic, smallish temple of Athena Polias (which means "protectress of the city"), he built a much larger one for the same goddess. It was called *Hekatompedon*, which means "one hundred feet long," but it was even bigger, at about 150 feet in length. The older temple, however, was not demolished at that time. On the contrary, it is believed that Pisistratus commissioned some renovations and improvements. Pisistratus's sons, who ruled Athens for a few years after their father's death, commissioned an expansion of the temple and a new decoration, adding a peristyle and statues to the pediment. In its final version, the Hekatompedon had six columns on its short side and twelve on the long one.

Under Pisistratus or perhaps his successors, the first opulent entry to the Acropolis was built, namely a *Propylon* – an outer monumental gateway standing before a main entrance – on the Acropolis's western side. Some remains are visible to this day, both inside and outside of the more recent Propylaea commissioned by Pericles to the architect Mnesicles and never completed due to the outbreak of the Peloponnesian War in 431 BCE.

Pisistratus is said to have been a wise ruler who was also a lover of the arts. Domestically, he fathered several reforms, incentivizing small landowners at the expense of large estates, increasing trade, thus favoring the mercantile class's growth, and executing an extensive plan of public works. To be sure, he also deprived Athens' citizens of some of their civil liberties.

Under Cleisthenes, perhaps around 505 BCE, a new imposing temple was commissioned, to be built where the Parthenon of Pericles later rose. The Hekatompedon, enlarged and embellished by Pisistratus or soon after, was too obvious a tribute to past tyranny. To properly honor the goddess, but even more so for the good of Athens' people, a new, major temple was called for to substantiate the power and wisdom of the nascent democratic regime. The construction of the new temple, conventionally named the Ancient Parthenon, probably continued during the age of Miltiades and Themistocles. It was never completed, though, and it suffered the same fate as most of the buildings on the Acropolis: It was reduced to a pile of ruins by the Persians in 480 BCE.

When the Athenians retook possession of their city, almost everything they had previously built on the Acropolis was destroyed. Out of reverence for the old sacred shrines, instead of just getting rid of the ruins, they buried them on that same hill. Centuries later, archaeologists could bring to light the remains of many a temple that inhabitants of the Athens of Pericles and the great philosophers – the city's Classical period – had never seen. That included several female statues called the Korai of the Acropolis, discovered in the last quarter of the nineteenth century, which are believed to have been part of the courtyard of the temple of Athena Polias. Their varied and beautiful looks returned an attractive and intriguing image of Athenian women of the Pisistratid period.

It appears that at the time of Themistocles, so decisive as a general against the Persians but later ostracized (expelled from the city) and even sentenced to death, a new god was welcomed to the Acropolis. It was Pan, a semi-goat deity from the region of Arcadia, god of the wild, shepherds, and flocks, and companion of the nymphs. Legend had it that he had helped the Athenians at the Battle of Marathon – in

490 BCE – by rousing the troops.

Pericles, who ruled Athens from 460 BCE to his death in 429 BCE, was the man who launched the project of building an Acropolis made of marble on top of the old one, made of limestone and poros (a coarse limestone), by then in ruins. The first new building to rise was the Parthenon.

THE PARTHENON

In Pericles's mind, the Parthenon [see cover image] was both a tribute to the goddess Athena, who had protected the city during the trying times of the Persian Wars, and a symbol of Athens' power, capable of surviving that deadly threat and conquering its enemies, thus establishing its hegemony over Greece. The old temple's foundations were used to construct the new one. Out of concern for the embankment's strength, they were widened toward the north, moving the building away from the rock's southern edge. At the same time, the need for a more extended floor pushed the construction to the western edge of the base, too.

Construction began in 447 BCE under the supervision of three architects – Ictinus, Callicrates, and Mnesicles – and the temple was pretty much finished by 438 BCE. That year, the gigantic and incredibly expensive 40-foot-tall statue of the goddess

Athena Parthenos by the great Athenian sculptor Phidias was completed, a stunning work of art entirely covered in gold and marble. Six years later, Phidias also created the statue of Zeus at Olympia, similarly tall and wrapped in the same materials, which was considered one of the seven wonders of the ancient world.

The Parthenon is entirely built of Pentelic marble, a natural stone with soft shades of golden yellow characteristic of Greece. It is a peripteral octastyle Doric temple, which means that it is bounded by a single row of columns, with the shorter side of the building having eight of them, while the longer side boasts seventeen. Each column is 34 feet tall and 6 feet wide at the base. The building measures 228 feet in length by 101 feet in width, making it much bigger than the old Hekatompedon it was intended to replace.

The Parthenon was richly decorated, of course. The ninety-two metopes of the entablature (the space above the columns beneath the roof) were decorated in high reliefs by Phidias and his pupils. They depict scenes from the Gigantomachy – the fight between the Giants and the Olympians – on the eastern side; the Amazonomachy – the battle between the Greeks and the Amazons, which also symbolizes the victory against the Persians – on the western side; and the Centauromachy – the fight between Centaurs and Lapiths, two legendary folks of the Greek mythology – on the northern and southern sides. Additionally, there were other episodes from Athenian myths and the fall of Troy. Of the missing metopes, some are kept at the Acropolis Museum in Athens, and many others can be seen at the British Museum in London.

Both triangular pediments were filled with statues in Parian marble. In the eastern one, Athens' citizens and visitors could admire the birth of the goddess Athena from the head of her father Zeus, while the western one depicted the clash for the mastery over Athens and Attica between Athena, holding the olive branch, and Poseidon, creating the horse from water. The two pediments were only completed in 432 BCE.

After centuries during which the Acropolis had been, first and foremost, a fortress defended by mighty walls, the construction of the Parthenon profoundly changed its nature, making unmistakably a sanctuary of it. This august temple, Athens' most recognizable landmark, still towers above the Acropolis and the entire city at its feet, proudly carrying all the scars of a long past.

THE LATER ACROPOLIS

The magnificent Parthenon was only the beginning of Athens' holy mountain's regeneration. The next step was to build a monumental access to the site from its western side. The sumptuous Propylaea were conceived as an ornamental entrance, not a defensive structure, by architect Mnesicles. Built between 437 and 432 BCE in Doric and Ionic style, this building replaced the ancient Propylon from the time of Pisistratus, though it was never completed with its finishing touches. The access to the Acropolis was now through this majestic entrance flanked by six Doric columns, three on each side, each 29 feet tall. This monument's poor conditions are due to a massive explosion that occurred during the Ottoman domination, in 1640, when it was used as an ammunition deposit.

Another project commissioned by Pericles was his Odeon, a covered theater of 44,000 square feet built outside of the Acropolis's walls at its southeastern tip. It was built in 435 BCE right beside the Theatre of Dionysus, which, dating back to the first years of the fifth century BCE, is considered the world's oldest theatre and the prototype for all Greek theatres to come. The Theatre of Dionysus was capable of accommodating as many as 15,000 to 17,000 spectators in an open-air hemicycle and served as the main stage for every major artistic production of the time, be it tragedy – by such authors as Aeschylus, Sophocles, and Euripides – or comedy – by authors like Aristophanes and Menander. Today, only a few remnants are visible. The same is true of Pericles's Odeon, a spectacular space whose roof was supported by no less than ninety interior pillars in nine rows of ten pillars each. Much of the wood used in the Odeon's construction came from the ships taken from the Persians.

Near the Propylaea, another temple was erected sometime between 430 and 420 BCE by Callicrates. It's a real gem of a shrine, devoted to Athena Nike, goddess of victory. Nike is depicted as a winged female figure, hence her moniker of Winged Victory. Compared to the Parthenon, this temple is tiny, but it is well-preserved and is made of beautiful Pentelic marble with golden hues in the Ionic style. It has four 13-foot-tall free-standing columns on the front and four on the back. Along the entablature, a continuous frieze told the story of an important battle between Greek and Persian forces in the presence of the gods, probably the one at Marathon or the Battle of Plataea. Interestingly, the statue of the goddess was made of wood, but its wings, which were later stolen, were golden.

In 421 BCE, works commenced on rebuilding the temple of Athena Polias, destroyed by the Persians in 480 BCE. Commissioned under Alcibiades, it was completed in 406 BCE, after a six or seven-year hiatus caused by the Peloponnesian War. The temple has six Ionic columns on the east side, while on the west side, four semi-columns decorate a wall with large windows. To the south, the loggia of the caryatids, built against the main construction, hosts the tomb of King Cecrops, Athens' first mythological monarch. A caryatid is a column in the guise of a female sculpture, and there are six of them supporting the loggia's roof. But those are copies. Five of the original ones can be seen at the Acropolis Museum, while a sixth was taken by the British diplomat Thomas Bruce, 7th Earl of Elgin and 11th Earl of Kincardine, when he was ambassador to the Ottoman Empire at the beginning of the nineteenth century. It can be found in a gallery at the British Museum in London.

To the north side of the temple, there is another portico, with four columns in front and two on each side. From here, one enters the chamber dedicated to worshiping Poseidon and Erechtheus, Athens' sixth mythological king. The portico also hosts the pool of salt water created by Poseidon and connects to an open-air area called Pandroseion, where the olive tree of Athena, an altar of Zeus Herkeios (protector of the hearth), and the tomb of Pandrosos, one of Cecrops' daughters, were located. This temple boasted especially slender and elegant columns and was handsomely decorated. A motif of lotus flowers and palmettes runs along the walls of the temple's main body, and gilding was widely used to embellish the site. Much later, the temple got its name of Erechtheion as a tribute to King Erechtheus.

Other notable shrines on the rebuilt Acropolis included the sanctuary of Pandion, dedicated to Athens' fifth mythological king and Erechtheus's father, the sanctuary of Artemis Brauronia, patron goddess of pregnant women and childbirth, and the restored sanctuary of Zeus Polieus.

In the wake of such splendid rejuvenation happening on the plateau of the Acropolis, its slopes could not remain abandoned. Its southern slope, particularly, became the site of several significant architectural projects. To the south of the ancient sanctuary of Dionysus, near the eponymous theater, a second one was built between 421 and 415 BCE on commission from the Athenian politician and general Nicias, who had given a decisive contribution in achieving the Peace of Nicias between Athens and Sparta in 421 BCE that had put an end to the first half of the Peloponnesian War. Very little has survived of both shrines, but we know that the cult statue, made of gold and ivory, was a work by the sculptor Alcamenes. It is unknown whether the walls decorated with scenes from the myth of Dionysus belonged to the vestibule or the cell.

Around the same time, a wealthy citizen named Telemachus commissioned a shrine devoted to Asclepius, the god of medicine and doctors, whose symbol was the serpent-entwined staff still found in every medical emergency service to this day. It was built to the west of the Theater of Dionysus, and it had a square enclosure, a temple, and a 160-foot-long Doric stoa with a double gallery separated by a row of columns, built in the fourth century BCE. A small grotto with a water source that is believed to be curative was converted into a Christian chapel. In ancient times, the sick were placed in the portico, where it was believed that Asclepius would appear in a dream and heal them.

It is presumed that two additional sanctuaries were located to the west of Asclepius's sanctuary: a temple devoted to Themis, daughter to Uranus – the god who was the embodiment of the sky – and Gea, the primordial goddess from whom life itself originates, and one devoted to Aphrodite, goddess of beauty and love.

Much later, the southern slope of the Acropolis was completed with two other monuments: the Stoa of Eumenes and the Odeon of Herodes Atticus. The Stoa (a portico or covered pathway) of Eumenes, located between the Theater of Dionysus and the Odeon of Herodes Atticus, was built around 160 BCE for King Eumenes II of Pergamon. It was over 500 feet long and, not having any chambers where to conduct business, it was meant as a spacious walkway for the visitors of Dionysus's theatre and temple at its eastern end. Its arches were integrated into a defensive wall built in Byzantine times (around 1060 CE).

The well-preserved Odeon to the west of the Stoa was commissioned by the phenomenally wealthy Athenian politician and sophist Herodes Atticus to commemorate his late wife, the Roman citizen Annia Regilla. Built sometime between 161 and 174 CE, it originally had a wooden roof. It had a capacity of some 5,000 spectators and was mainly used as a venue for musical performances.

The Odeon of Herodes Atticus can be considered the swansong of the Classical Acropolis. After its completion, the decline began.

THE AREOPAGUS

Just to the northwest of the Acropolis lies another, lower hill: the Areopagus (the "hill of Ares"). Its name derives from Ares, son of Zeus and Hera, the goddess of women, marriage, and family. Legend has it that Ares, the god of war's more violent degeneration into plain bloodlust – later to be named Mars by the Romans – was accused by Poseidon of killing his son Halirrhothius after the latter had raped Ares's daughter Alcippe. Tried before a court of fellow divinities on this hill, he was acquitted since Alcippe confirmed the charges against Halirrhothius, and there were no other eyewitnesses to hear. The only thing certain is that a temple was devoted to Ares on this spot from ancient times.

Historically, the Areopagus was initially the site where Athens' council of supreme magistrates met, presided by the king, to judge blood crimes and delicts against the cult and supervise the state's administration and the execution of the laws. With the rise of the first democratic institutions, notably the Boule established by Cleisthenes in 508 BCE, this assembly's importance gradually declined. By 462 BCE, under the archon Ephialtes, its role was reduced to dealing only with crimes relating to sacrilege and voluntary manslaughter. In later years, the body regained importance with the decline of democracy and the rise of Hellenistic civilization.

A trial would typically be conducted as follows: the accuser presented the complaint to the *Basileus* (the archon king), who would forbid the defendant from entering any sacred shrines and temples for the time of the entire trial. After three months, the parties came before the tribunal with great solemnity and took an oath to tell the truth. The witnesses did the same. The accuser stood on a stone called the "stone of truthfulness," while the accused stood on one called the "stone of conceit." Interestingly, in the event of a split jury – with an equal number of votes to convict and to acquit – the accused was free to go.

A Christian name is also deeply connected to the Areopagus's history: that of the apostle Paul. Paul reached Athens on his second missionary journey, most likely in 49 CE. At that time, Athens was nothing more than a pale copy of the powerful city of Pericles and the great philosophers. It was part of the Roman province of Achaia, and instead of the 300,000 inhabitants of its golden era, it numbered perhaps 10,000 to 20,000. And yet, it still retained some of its former drawing power, at least in cultural terms. Paul, intent on spreading the "good news" of the Gospel as widely as possible throughout the empire, could not skip this glorious capital of the ancient world.

In Athens, Paul was greeted by a seemingly endless number of pagan temples. In his eyes, they all were meaningless tributes to false idols. As was his custom everywhere he went, the first place where Paul preached the Gospel was the synagogue, where he always tried to convince his fellow Jews that the Messiah had come. But he also loved to mingle with people of different faiths in the Agora, Athens' main public square, where he met Athenians from every walk of life who never shied away from a healthy argument. Epicureanism and Stoicism were the dominant philosophical trends of the time, and Paul was invited to speak at the Areopagus to plead his case.

He was an educated man familiar with Greek poetry and philosophy, so he had no difficulty captivating the audience with his argument about God. Only when he introduced the belief in a Messiah who died on the cross and was resurrected from death did the listening crowd decide they had heard enough. To Greek ears, the idea of bodily resurrection after one's death was pure nonsense. More than anything, it was not a desirable fate. Hence, they dismissed him, telling him mockingly that they would listen to him another time.

Today, nothing is left to be seen on this boulder-strewn hill, except for an engraved plaque that bears the inscription of Paul's famous sermon, as recorded in chapter 17 of the Book of Acts.

THE AGORA

The Agora has always been Athens' main square, where most open-air city life happened, just as in every other Greek city's agora. Athens' ancient Agora lies just north of the Areopagus, in an area rich in remains of monuments of the past.

As a square market, the Agora was the city's economic life center. The traders set up their shacks there and carried on their small business under the supervision of magistrates who ensured the goods' quality respected the required standard and checked weights and measures. Barbers and perfumers offered cheerful hospitality in their shops to those in the mood for chitchat. Vendors were arranged and grouped according to their merchandise. Bankers sat in front of their tables, where coins, registers, documents, and valuables were piled, always surrounded by a crowd of businessmen and onlookers.

To avoid getting lost in the big square, country

people met at determined points, a well-established habit even registered in official documents. The maximum influx of people occurred between nine and noon, when as many as twenty thousand people could roam Athens' main square. Just like any other place filled with a bustling crowd, the Agora also attracted a great number of vagabonds, crooks, and idlers. According to famed playwright Aristophanes (446-386 BCE), nothing of value could be learned in the Agora, and in his comedy *The Clouds*, he advised all well-mannered young men to keep away from it, just as every "honest" woman would think twice before venturing into the crowd. Therefore, it was customary for Athenian husbands to personally get their supplies or to entrust a slave with grocery shopping.

The Agora was also the civic and religious heart of the town's life. On major religious feasts, the solemn processions' starting point was in this square. For instance, the closing procession of the Panathenaic festival, ancient Athens' most important religious and civil holiday in honor of Athena Polias, which included several sporting events, started from a sanctuary called Leokorion to finish at the goddess' temple on the Acropolis. Furthermore, whoever had been sentenced for a serious offense or was awaiting judgment in a grave case was barred from entering the city's temples, including the sacred places in the Agora.

Actually, only Athens' citizens were at home in this all-important public space, and only if they possessed political and civil rights. Foreigners were barely tolerated here, and they could not engage in petty trade unless they paid a special tax after getting specific authorization. Citizens, on the other hand, enjoyed some of the authority that the head of a family has in his house. In fact, they had a duty to prevent murderers, outlaws, and the ungodly from accessing the square and to detain them and deliver them to the magistrate to be put in chains. In his dialogue titled *The Laws*, Plato even threatens the harshest penalties for anyone who does not make immediate and forceful use of this authority.

Of all the squares in the Greek world, Athens' Agora was by far the most famous and significant. Unfortunately, while we possess numerous noteworthy literary testimonies, historical relics are scarce and heavily damaged. Nowadays, very little can be seen of the multitude of monuments and buildings once dotting the square. We know that most of the city's main public buildings overlooked the square. Its central area was paved, adorned with statues of ancient heroes and worthy citizens, herms, several fountains, olive trees and sycamores, and various porches. Among them, the most famous one was the *Stoa Poikile*, the "painted porch," from which the Stoics derived their name since that was where the students of Zeno of Citium, the founder of the Stoic philosophical school, gathered for their discussions.

Many public offices were arranged around the square, including the one where the Boule met, the Temple of Cybele, where the National Archive was housed, the tribunals, and many residences of various magistrates. In the *Stoa Basileios*, the "royal porch," the fundamental laws of the city-state were displayed, and here all magistrates took a solemn oath to observe and enforce them. Several temples and altars were located in the Agora, too. An Altar of the Twelve Gods (the Olympians), commissioned by Pisistratus – a grandson of the earlier tyrant by the same name – marked the city's geographical center, from where the distances from Athens were measured.

Most public buildings were located in the square's southern part, which was the center of administrative life. The merchants occupied the northern and western areas, the market in a stricter sense.

Athens' Agora was also the playing field of one of history's greatest philosophers: Socrates. Born in Athens in 470 or 469 BCE, Socrates had a full life as a philosopher, soldier, and politician. Between 432 and 422 BCE, he took part in the siege of Potidaea and the battles of Delium and Amphipolis as a hoplite (foot soldier). He never aspired to get involved in the matters of the state, but he could not refuse to be part of the Boule when drawn. As a philosopher, he never wrote anything. His method was based on dialogue with his interlocutors. According to Socrates, truth cannot simply be taught; it must be generated from inside you. Thus, he acted like a midwife helping his students give birth to it.

He was also a fierce enemy of tradition. He would not accept any principle that did not justify itself by simple reason but instead needed to invoke obedience to a higher authority. This was what ultimately got him into trouble. In 399 BCE, Socrates was accused by Anytus, a wealthy Athenian politician, Meletus, a philosopher on Anytus's payroll, and Lycon, a professional rhetorician, of acting illicitly, not believing in the gods that the city's inhabitants worshiped and introducing new divinities (a charge of impiety), besides also corrupting Athens' youth. For such misdeeds, a death sentence was the most likely outcome.

Our knowledge of Socrates's response stems from Plato's *The Apology*. Plato, who later became one of history's greatest philosophers in his own right, was Socrates's most gifted pupil. According to Plato's account, Socrates justified himself in a poised, good-natured, sometimes even ironic way at his trial. He explained his reasons, but he would not invoke the clemency of the court – five hundred Athenian citizens – as was customary, in the hope for leniency. He was declared guilty by a majority of sixty votes. Following the Attic procedure, he was asked to propose a penalty in alternative to the one requested by the prosecution, but he replied that, for his merits toward the city, he believed he should be maintained at public expense in the Prytaneion, the seat of government next to the Boule. Unsurprisingly, he was then sentenced to death.

The execution of the sentence was delayed by about a month for ritual reasons, allowing Socrates a chance to flee the city according to an escape plan by his disciple and friend Crito, but he famously refused. He chose to respect those laws that were sacred to him to the bitter end, even if that meant taking his own life. Surrounded by friends and pupils, after discussing the matter of death and the afterlife with them – his last philosophical gift – he drank the hemlock and died peacefully. His shining example of uncompromising moral fortitude has intrigued historians and philosophers ever since.

THE TEMPLE OF
HEPHAESTUS

A well-preserved testament to Athens' former glory is the Temple of Hephaestus, or *Hephaisteion*, which stands on a small hill called *Kolonos Agoraios* on the western side of the Agora. It is one of the best-preserved Doric temples in the world. It is also the only ancient temple in all of Greece to retain its roof. Contrary to most other Classical temples, it doesn't appear to have been built on top of the ruins of a more ancient one. The temple was also known as the *Theseion*, a name given to it because of the belief that the remains of the mythical hero Theseus were buried in the temple.

Hephaestus was a god of uncertain origins. The ancients were unsure if he should be considered a son of Zeus and Hera, just as Ares, or if Hera had autogenerated him all by herself to take revenge on her spouse for his countless affairs. Either way, one of his parents was said to have hurled him to earth, which explained why he was crippled and only able to walk with the aid of a cane. He was the god of fire, blacksmiths' forges, engineering, and metallurgy. As such, he was the official blacksmith of the heroes' armor, cups, and treasures. He also made most of the magnificent objects used by the gods. He was worshiped in all Ancient Greek cities where craft activities were found.

The Temple of Hephaestus is 129 feet long and 55 feet wide, with thirty-four Doric columns. Its construction began in 449 BCE, a couple of years before the Parthenon's, probably on a project by Ictinus or Callicrates, who later worked on the more famous "cousin" too. Inside, in the temple's cell, stood the bronze cult statues of Athena and Hephaestus, now lost, realized by the sculptor Alcamenes. The two pediments are also lost, but it is believed they showed the birth of Athena (on the eastern façade) and a Gigantomachy (on the western façade). The entablature was decorated with sixty-eight metopes, twenty-four on each of the temple's long sides and ten on both short ones, of which only eighteen must have been sculptured, while the other fifty were painted. They depicted the labors of Heracles (Hercules in Rome) – one of Ancient Greece's most famous myths – and the ventures of Theseus. On the temple's inside, there were friezes along the architrave of both the cell's *pronaos* (the space before the cell) and *opisthodomos* (the space behind it).

The temple was certainly closed during the

persecution of pagans starting in the fifth century. It was then converted into a Catholic church dedicated to the memory of St. George, patron saint of England, toward the end of the seventh century.

THE ROMAN AGORA AND HADRIAN'S LIBRARY

To the east of the original Agora and the north of the Acropolis, there is a second public square in the Plaka district called the Roman Agora. In 146 BCE, the Roman Republic annexed Greece to its territories, thus taking over the administration of Athens. In 19 BCE, Rome's first emperor, Octavianus Augustus, decided to give the ancient metropolis a new market square along the lines of the Forum Romanum the Romans used to build in every conquered city.

Upon completing eight years of work, the square occupied a rectangular area of 364 by 321 feet and was surrounded by porticos, where all kinds of trade took place. It had two monumental accesses: the Gate of Athena Archegetis on its western side, partially still standing, and a propylaeum in the east. In the second century CE, the Roman emperor Hadrian commissioned a vast public building called Hadrian's Library. Despite the destruction following the sack of Athens by the Heruli in 267 CE, substantial remains of the western façade and part of the entrance can still be admired today.

The Heruli were a Germanic people originally from Scandinavia who, in the third century CE, used to raid towns and villages in some provinces of the Roman Empire. In 267 CE, at the height of their power, they even conquered Byzantium and sacked several Greek cities, Athens among them. Two years later, they were crushingly defeated by Claudius II Gothicus, the first of Rome's Danubian emperors, in a battle near Naissus (modern-day Niš, in Serbia).

Inside, Hadrian's Library consisted of a vast, four-sided portico with one hundred columns overall. An elongated water basin occupied the building's center, probably surrounded by a garden enhanced with plentiful statues. The long sides of the portico boasted three exedras each (in architecture, an exedra is a recess, usually semicircular, surmounted by a half-dome, often but not always placed on a building's façade), with two columns gracing their entrances.

The library rooms were located at the end of the portico, on the opposite side from the entrance. The central one, which was the largest, opened onto the portico with four columns and had walls decorated with columns and two orders of niches to house the volumes (which were papyrus rolls). It was flanked by two smaller rooms, opening onto the portico with two columns. The library also had an auditorium fitted with bleachers.

A well-preserved testimony of ancient times is the Tower of the Winds, in the square's southeastern corner, also called the *Horologion* (literally, in Greek, "what tells the time," i.e., a clock). The Tower is an octagonal building made of Pentelic marble, 42 feet tall and 26 feet in diameter, built around 50 BCE, likely on a design by the Syrian astronomer Andronicus of Cyrrhus. Originally, it was topped by a weathervane in the form of Triton, a marine deity born from Poseidon and the Nereid Amphitrite, a sea nymph. The Tower's water clock was driven by a brook from the Acropolis called Clepsydra. The Tower also served as a planetarium, outfitted with an instrument capable of recording the movement of the sun, the moon, and the five planets known at the time. At the top of the building, eight friezes depict the gods of the winds, called *Anemoi*. The Winds are portrayed as four adults and four youngsters, flying with wings spread. In their hands, they hold the symbolic gifts of the season in which each of them typically blows.

THE ARCH OF HADRIAN

Another legacy of Roman rule over Athens is the Arch of Hadrian, also known as Hadrian's Gate, to the east of the Acropolis.

Hadrian was Rome's fourteenth emperor from August 117 to July 138 CE. He succeeded his predecessor Trajan, under whom the empire had reached its maximum geographical expansion, as his adoptive son. He was a great admirer of Greek culture and traveled extensively during his reign. He was more interested in consolidating the empire's borders than expanding them, which explains the construction of that impressive defensive structure called Hadrian's Wall in England, to the south of Scotland, to protect the Roman province of Britannia from the raiding Pictish tribes.

The commissioner of this beautiful gate is unknown, but it is believed that it was completed on time for Hadrian's visit to Athens, a city with a special place in his heart, to inaugurate the Temple of Olympian Zeus nearby, in 131 or 132 CE. The arch is made of the usual Pentelic marble found everywhere in the city's monuments, and it was built without the help of cement and mortar, with only rivets used to hold together the marble blocks. The structure is almost 60 feet tall, 44 feet wide, and 7½ feet deep, with a 21-foot-wide opening at the base. Both sides of the central passageway were decorated with a raised rectangular-based Corinthian column protruding from the wall, which is now gone.

The monument's upper part consists of a structure of four pillars framing three openings, surmounted by an architrave, and with an additional two columns supporting the central pediment. The capitals of the pillars and columns are in Corinthian style. A frieze at the top of the gate's lower part shows an inscription. The one on the northwest side, looking toward the Acropolis, reads: "This is Athens, the ancient city of Theseus." On the opposite side, looking toward the Temple of Olympian Zeus, the frieze reads: "This is the city of Hadrian, and not of Theseus." It is not entirely clear if those inscriptions were meant to separate the old, Classical city founded by Theseus from the newer districts owed to the emperor's influence or if they were supposed to mean that Athens as a whole, once the city of Theseus, was now Hadrian's.

Considering its age and the shape in which most Ancient Athens monuments have reached us, the Arch of Hadrian is in a remarkably good state of preservation. The same cannot be said of the Temple

of Olympian Zeus, of which only a few scattered columns survive.

THE TEMPLE OF
OLYMPIAN ZEUS

For a long time, this temple with a troubled history was the grandest temple of the Hellenistic world, much larger even than the Parthenon. Also called the *Olympieion*, its construction started in 515 BCE on the ruins of an earlier temple, in the waning years of the tyranny of Peisistratus the Young. Construction was halted a few years later when the last tyrant was overthrown, and democratic governance was slowly established. For many years, nobody wanted to resume work on the temple for fear of legitimizing the city's tyrannical rulers.

So, part of the temple stood unfinished for over three centuries until Antiochus IV Epiphanes, a Seleucid king, finally completed it in 174 BCE. But it took another three centuries to actually finish this magnificent and towering building, after the emperor Hadrian, during his visit to Athens in 124 or

125 CE, had given the decisive impulse. The emperor returned in 132 CE to dedicate the temple to Zeus, the king of the gods on Mount Olympus (hence the moniker "Olympian"). The temple stood on a gigantic platform measuring 354 by 134 feet. It had one hundred and four Corinthian columns, which were 56 feet tall and had a diameter of 6½ feet at the base. Today, only fifteen of those columns still stand, while another one lies on the ground in pieces after being struck by lightning during a heavy thunderstorm in 1852.

Unfortunately, as happened to many other of Athens' ancient buildings, the Olympieion was later plundered by the barbarians and subsequently used as a quarry for its building materials; thus, no part of its interior survived. After Emperor Theodosius had banned the worship of pagan idols throughout the empire in 391/392 CE, the city's Christians were allowed to incorporate some of the building materials into a basilica constructed nearby.

THE PANATHENAIC
STADIUM AND GAMES

To the east of Hadrian's Gate and the scant remains of the Olympieion lies this gigantic structure, the only stadium in the world built entirely of Pentelic marble, capable of holding up to 70,000 spectators.

For the record, this is not where the Olympic Games of antiquity took place. Those were organized every four years in the city of Olympia, in the Ilia region at the western end of the Peloponnese peninsula, starting with the first edition in 776 BCE. It must be said that some form of competitive activity had already existed in Mesopotamia, Egypt, and Crete centuries before the first ancient Olympic Games were held. However, those sporting events were mostly sporadic and lacked precise rules; thus, we can safely argue that no other people nurtured the idea of athletic competition as comprehensibly as the Ancient Greeks. That competitive spirit was probably born in connection with religion and its rituals but soon became even more prominent to fulfill military training needs.

Soldiers' physical preparedness was a key component of any army hoping to succeed on the battlefield, so it made sense to ask those citizens who could one day be requested to fight to keep in shape to the best of their ability. Racing increased speed and endurance, jumping benefited agility, discus and javelin throw built muscle strength, and disciplines such as boxing and the very popular wrestling prepared the future soldier for hand-to-hand fighting on the battlefield. In that respect, it is well established that the Greeks of the pre-Classical era (considered to run approximately from 800 to 500 BCE) were the first to develop large-scale athletic games on a regular basis, defined by a complex protocol aimed at creating great solemnity for the whole event.

The intent of all athletic competitions in Ancient Greece was to glorify the gods. In the context of a polytheistic cult, the institution of competitive games was meant to honor them through a rigorous ceremonial. Competitions were more a religious ritual than a sporting event as we know them today, to the point that a winning athlete was believed to get a step closer to divinity himself. All over Greece, the *poleis* (city-states) hosted hundreds of games of local or regional relevance. This kind of celebration always had two main elements: the religious rites made of processions, sacrifices, votive offerings, and prayers on the one side, and the competitions proper, on the other. Beyond the sporting events in several disciplines, musical contests were customary, as well as contests in rhetoric, theatre arts, dance, and painting.

Pierre de Coubertin, the father of the modern Olympic Games, thus expressed his philosophy: "The important thing in life is not the triumph but the struggle; the essential thing is not to have won but to have fought well." The Ancient Greeks couldn't agree less. To them, winning was the only thing that mattered, faithful to the traditional model of the heroic man. There was no podium in Greece's games, since there was nothing to celebrate in coming second or third in a competition. Victory alone gave glory and was a source of pride for the champion, while defeat was considered infamy, or at least a great dishonor. We can safely say that the modern concept of fair play never crossed the Ancient Greeks' minds.

* * *

The games in Athens, called Panathenaic Games or *Panathenaea*, were the best-known and most successful ones. According to tradition, their founder was Erichthonius, Athens' fourth mythological king. Historians, though, believe the first edition of this festival took place in 566 BCE, under the eponymous archon (the city's chief magistrate, after whom the year was named) Hippocleides. Initially, competitions were reserved for Athens' citizens only, but were opened to athletes from allied poleis by Pisistratus in 528 BCE. The festival was a multi-day event held annually, with a longer, more important edition every four years (the Great Panathenaea). Chances are Theodosius's edicts in 390/391 CE put an end to this kind of games, which always included pagan rites and sacrifices to the gods.

The Panathenaic Games were dedicated to Athena and took place toward the end of July, when Athens was traditionally thought to have been founded. The Great ones were scheduled in the third year of each Olympiad, the four-year cycle into which all athletic competitions in Greece were organized. The festival included musical and acting competitions, hosted in the majestic Odeon of Pericles after its inauguration in 435 BCE, as well as a regatta and a beauty contest of sorts. It should be noted that physical beauty was a much-respected quality in Ancient Greece, where, far from being a random attribute, it was considered a sign of divine benevolence. Athletics competitions were held in the imposing Panathenaic Stadium before tens of thousands of cheering spectators.

The start of the competitions was preceded by a procession through the main streets of Athens. The frieze that decorates the Parthenon's cell describes the parade's composition in detail: the train was opened by a ship towed on wheels, escorted by young girls carrying amphorae filled with wine. The oxen intended for sacrifice came next, followed by the heralds at the head of the delegations from

Athens, the colonies, and the allied poleis. The city's authorities were part of the procession, too, be it the members of the Boule, the archons, the strategoi, and the treasurers. The parade was closed by children carrying amphorae, soldiers, and armed knights. Some elderly people also took part in the Panathenaic procession. Each tribe selected its representatives, and the delegation with the best-looking elders was rewarded.

The procession's final destination was the Acropolis. Here, some girls of noble families dressed the statue of the goddess Athena in a gorgeous peplos. This was followed by the swearing-in ceremony of athletes and judges, the latter chosen from each of the ten Athenian tribes and appointed for four years. The rites ended with the sacrifice of one hundred oxen (the *hecatomb*) and the final banquet, attended by all the participants. Once the formalities were over, the nine-day festivities began. All events held in the Olympic Games were also scheduled in Athens, including chariot and horse races. Contestants were divided into two and, later, three different age categories.

Apart from the glory, winners received cash prizes and some 1,300 large vases known as Panathenaic amphorae, beautifully decorated and filled with oil. Oil was the most valuable product of Attica, so much so that all olive trees belonged to the state, not private citizens. Every amphora contained roughly twenty liters of oil and was worth about twelve drachmas, a not-insignificant amount of money. The vases depicted scenes from the competition won by the honored athlete, painted in black on a red background, and an image of Athena equipped with a helmet, shield, and spear on the opposite side. Panathenaic amphorae were found in places far away from Greece, which hints that the contest winners were allowed to sell them for profit.

THE ROMAN BATHS
AT ZAPPEION

Not far from the Arch of Hadrian, along Amalias Avenue, lies a small archaeological site that tells about the Romans' influence on the city: the Roman Baths. They are located in what once was a bucolic area just outside the old city walls, known as a worship site for several deities. Thanks to the Ilisos river flowing nearby, it had plentiful running waters and lush vegetation, which made it an ideal place to build the thermal baths Roman occupiers liked to create everywhere they went.

When the city walls were expanded under Hadrian, the site became part of Athens' inner city. Private and public buildings rose in this area, including some sanctuaries. Toward the end of the third century CE, after the looting by the Heruli, the Baths were finally built, most likely under the emperor Diocletian. The thermae were discovered during excavations related to the construction of Athens' subway and were opened to the public in 2003, after renovation, preservation, and roofing works.

THE ACADEMY

One of Athens' most stately buildings is a modern one. Built between 1859 and 1885, when the project was finally completed, it was inaugurated in 1926 as Greece's most prestigious research institution, operating under the country's Ministry of Education in three distinct fields of knowledge: Natural Sciences, Arts and Letters, and Moral and Political Sciences. It was built in the neoclassical style, with two rows of Ionic columns gracing its façade. It was designed by the Danish architect Theophil Hansen, whose brother Christian Hansen designed the university's building nearby.

The Academy stands at the center of a trio of buildings widely considered to be amongst the most beautiful examples of neoclassical architecture. In addition to the Academy, there's the headquarters of the University of Athens, officially founded in April 1837, to its right, and the National Library, opened in 1903 after fifteen years' work, to its left. Two majestic pillars, 76 feet tall, tower over the Academy's entrance. A statue of Athena tops the left one, while Apollo, holding his lyre (a musical instrument with seven strings the god was said to have invented), stands on top of the right one, both realized by the sculptor Leonidas Drosis.

At the top of the stairs giving access to the building's forecourt, two 8-foot-tall statues greet visitors. Designed by Drosis and executed by the Italian sculptor Piccarelli, they depict Athens' famed philosophers Plato on the left and Socrates on the right, both seated in a pensive attitude. Besides being a well-earned tribute to two of Athens' best-known titans of Western philosophy, the statues also recall the obvious historical roots of the Academy's name, i.e., Plato's Academy.

After Socrates's death, Plato, the great philosopher's most brilliant pupil, left Athens for a series of travels. After returning from Syracuse, in Sicily, where he had tried to persuade the tyrant Dionysius the Elder to govern according to justice (unsuccessfully), he founded his school around 387 BCE. Its name, *Akademeia*, came from a grove on the outskirts of Athens that was dedicated to the Greek mythological hero Academus, where Plato gave his lectures.

Founded by Plato as a school for the training of politicians – who, at that time, were requested to understand the basics of rational thought – the Academy was characterized by subjects such as mathematics and dialectics, which the great philosopher considered essential to a politician's education, as expounded in his *Republic*. Plato's method was based on debates. Usually, the master would pose a philosophical problem, inviting his students to put forward solutions which were then subjected to examination and refutation attempts, aiming to identify the most reliable and convincing thesis. Four debates have been handed down concerning the movements of observable planets, the reality of ideas, the nature of principles (the building blocks of reality), and the relationship between pleasure and the good.

The Academy's most famous student was Aristotle, who, after Plato died in 347 BCE, left Athens for several teaching assignments in the Eastern Mediterranean world. In 342 BCE, he was called to Pella by King Philip II of Macedonia to be his son Alexander's tutor. After three years, Alexander had to leave to participate in his father's military expeditions, the first step in a career that would make him Alexander the Great.

SYNTAGMA SQUARE

Reachable both by bus and metro, Syntagma Square is modern Athens' most important public space. Located not far from the Roman Baths, it has a surface area of about 270,000 square feet and is also known as Constitution Square. That's because, on 3 September 1843, the people of Athens came together in this square to ask King Otto to accept the formulation of a new Constitution for the Greek people. Otto, a German prince of the House Wittelsbach, had been appointed king of Greece by the Conference of London in 1832, when the Great Powers had decided to create a new, independent Kingdom of Greece under the protection of France, Russia, and the United Kingdom. But Otto, who ruled as an absolute monarch, was never loved by his subjects. In September 1843, he had to introduce several constitutional reforms, bowing to an insurrection led by Dimitrios Kallergis, an infantry colonel, and Ioannis Makriyannis, a revolutionary leader, with the support of Athens' population.

To the east of the square lie two important landmarks: the Hellenic Parliament Building, formerly Athens' Royal Palace, and the Tomb of the Unknown Soldier.

The Royal Palace was built between 1836 and 1842, and the royal couple – Otto and his spouse Amalia – took possession of it in July 1843, shortly before the brief and mostly bloodless revolution. In 1863, King George I – a Dane – followed Otto on the throne and occupied the Palace until 1913, when he was assassinated by a Greek anarchist, in the context of the First Balkan War (from 8 October 1912 to 30 May 1913). The Palace is situated on the fringes of the splendid National Gardens, whose development was somewhat of a pet project for Queen Amalia. Since 1935, the building houses both chambers of the Greek Parliament.

Before the large staircase leading to the Palace's entrance lies the Tomb of the Unknown Soldier. It was inaugurated on 25 March 1932, Greece's Independence Day, celebrating the start of the War of Independence against the Ottomans in 1821. Like all similar monuments around the world, it is constantly guarded by a detachment of soldiers dressed in traditional and eye-catching uniforms, called the Evzones. The changing of the guard, which takes place every hour on the hour, always attracts a crowd of onlookers. The monument's sides bear the inscription of Pericles's Funeral Oration, delivered in 430 BCE (see the first chapter of this book).

On the square's northern side is the Hotel Grand Bretagne, now part of Marriott's Luxury Collection, Athens' most storied five-star hotel. Dignitaries, celebrities, and the ultra-wealthy from all over the world have always loved this establishment affording spectacular views of the Parliament, the Acropolis, and the towering Lycabettus Hill not far away. The adjoining Hotel King George belongs to the same hotel group and is equally impressive (and expensive).

MONASTIRAKI SQUARE

Monastiraki, considered Athens' more popular heart, is both a square and a city district. Situated just north of the Acropolis, of which it offers a nice view from below, it is best known for hosting a buzzing flea market. The area is also one of Athens' main shopping districts, and many local taverns and restaurants dot the streets all around the square. But shopping isn't the only reason to go.

A bit below street level, in the middle of the square, sits a charming, smallish Byzantine church from the tenth century, the Panagia Pantanassa Church. It is all that remains of the ancient monastery that gave its name to the square and harbors a remarkable early icon of the Virgin Mary.

The square's southern corner is occupied by the Tzistarakis Mosque, which is a reminder of the Ottomans' domination over the city which lasted from 1456, when the cultural capital of Ancient Greece fell into the hands of Mehmet II – the Ottoman Empire's seventh sultan and conqueror of Constantinople three years earlier – to 1829, when most of the Greek territory was freed from the Ottoman invader in the wake of the Greek War of Independence. The mosque was built in 1759 under the city's Ottoman governor, Mustafa Agha Tzistarakis, and now serves as a branch of the Greek Folk Art Museum, showcasing above all collections of ceramics.

One of Athens' most ancient metro stations, opened in May 1895, can also be found in the square, hosted in a beautiful building. The station's name was Monastirion until 1976, before being renamed Monastiraki, and there are still signs bearing the old name inside the station, which might confuse some tourists. The underground itself can be considered a tourist attraction in its own right, being widely considered one of the most beautiful in the world, with its stations entirely done in marble and granite and more than a few archaeological finds on display.

In walking distance from Monastiraki Square are two Christian churches that are worth a visit: the Metropolitan Cathedral of Athens, also known as Metropolis, which is the seat of the archbishop and Greece's most important house of worship, and the tiny Church of St. Eleutherios, also known as Little Metropolis, right beside. The Little Metropolis is a small Orthodox church built on top of the ruins of an ancient pagan temple sometime after 1436 in the typical Byzantine cross-in-square layout, with extensive use of reused material coming from earlier buildings. Only one of the many frescos that originally decorated its interior survives today.

The Metropolitan Cathedral, also belonging to the Orthodox Church, was built between 1842 and 1862 to replace the ancient Metropolis next door as the cathedral for the Metropolitan of Athens. The first stone was laid on Christmas Day, 1842, in the presence of King Otto and Queen Amalia. After twenty years of work under three different architects – first, Theophil Hansen, followed by Demetrio Zezos, and lastly, the Frenchman François Boulanger after Zezos died in 1857 – it was consecrated to the Annunciation of the Virgin Mary on 21 May 1862. The church is 130 feet long, 65 feet wide, and 80 feet tall, and it was necessary to demolish the astounding number of seventy-two churches to collect enough building material to erect its massive walls.

The cathedral's exterior is done in a simple yet elegant late Byzantine style, with two slender bell towers, one of which has a clock, framing its main façade. Visitors are greeted by three arches supported by modern-looking columns surmounted by a mosaic depicting the Annunciation, with the Archangel Gabriel reaching the Virgin Mary in a garden with a fountain at its center. The small square in front of the cathedral's entrance hosts the statues of Constantine XI Palaeologus, the last Byzantine emperor who was killed by the Ottomans during the fall of Constantinople in 1453, and Damaskinos Papandreou, who was archbishop of Athens and also regent of the exiled King George II from 1944 to 1946.

Inside, two coffins contain the remains of two saints venerated by the Orthodox Church: Patriarch

Gregory V, killed by the Turks in 1821, and Saint Philothei of Athens, a Greek Orthodox religious sister who was beaten to death in 1588 by four Ottoman mercenaries who had broken into the monastery at Patisia – a neighborhood of Athens – where she lived. Her silver casket is a wonderful goldsmithing work, made in the nineteenth century to replace the first, simpler one from 1589. The saint's mortal remains are visible through a large glass opening at the shrine's top.

THE PLAKA

The Plaka is one of Athens' oldest and most central districts, located just east of Monastiraki Square and surrounding the Acropolis from the north and the east. Despite attracting countless tourists, this district is still worth a visit, with its narrow and often labyrinthine cobbled streets and its beautiful nineteenth-century neoclassical houses, souvenir shops, jewelry stores, restaurants, and open-air cafés.

Now mostly a pedestrian area, this is where the region's first inhabitants are thought to have settled down as early as seven thousand years ago. The district also boasts some historical attractions, such as the Roman Agora and several lovely Byzantine churches dating back to the tenth to the twelfth century, some of them tiny.

At the Plaka's southern tip, a stone's throw away from the Acropolis, stands the Choragic Monument of Lysicrates, the only surviving example of this special type of memorial. A *choregos* was a moneyed citizen appointed to the public office of financing and organizing a lyric or dramatic choir to participate in the Great Dionysia, a yearly festival of comedy, tragedy, and satirical drama attended by visitors from throughout Greece. After winning the edition of 334 BCE, Lysicrates commissioned this monument to glorify himself in perpetuity.

LYCABETTUS HILL

One of Athens' seven hills (just like Rome's!), the Lycabettus is its tallest, being 911 feet high. Its top is the perfect vantage point to enjoy a spectacular view over the whole city in every direction, including the Acropolis and the Parthenon to its southwest, with the sea in the background.

As legend has it, the goddess Athena was intent on hauling a gigantic boulder to lay on top of the Acropolis because she wanted a temple to her name nearer to the sky when she received a piece of news that surprised her enough to cause her to let the rock fall, thus creating the hill. The great number of wolves once roaming these slopes, covered by thick wood vegetation, gave it its name, which means "hill of the wolves." Nowadays, birds, to the tune of more than sixty different species, and Greek tortoises are the hill's main inhabitants.

On the top of the hill, which can be reached by

foot or with the help of a cable car called Teleferik that runs through a tunnel, there is a panoramic platform from which to take in the city below. This is also where a temple to Zeus once stood, now replaced by a lovely, white Orthodox chapel named after Saint George. A large water tank serving Hadrian's aqueduct was located on the hill's south slope, some remains of which were still visible up to the eighteenth century.

To bask in the most incredible explosion of red shades, climb the Lycabettus right before sunset; after the sun goes down, Athens will unfold before you, shining a thousand lights.

MUSEUMS

There are many museums in Athens, and at least two are not to be missed: the Acropolis Museum and the National Archaeological Museum. But several others are worth a visit, depending on your interests.

The Acropolis Museum

Inaugurated only in 2009, this is now Athens' most important and most visited museum. The building, a project by Swiss architect Bernard Tschumi in collaboration with Greek architect Michalis Fotiadis, is a wonder of contemporary architecture in and by itself. It was built on top of an archaeological site using steel, glass, and concrete and has a total surface area of 270,000 square feet, of which 150,000 are devoted to the exhibition space proper.

A few steps away from the Theatre of Dionysus,

just south of the Acropolis, the Acropolis Museum is a veritable treasure trove of ancient artifacts and sculptures, together with a number of replicas of temples and shrines once found on the namesake hill nearby. Furthermore, visitors can admire sections of the archaeological site beneath the floor through glass panels located both outside and inside the building. The exhibition is divided into five main thematic areas: the slopes of the Acropolis, the Parthenon, the Archaic Acropolis, the Classical Acropolis, and other collections.

The museum's last floor, slightly tilted relative to the rest of the building, has the same dimensions and orientation as the Parthenon, just a quarter of a mile away. The full Parthenon frieze is replicated in this hall.

The National Archaeological Museum

In this museum, you are granted a full immersion into the whole of Greece's long history, starting from prehistoric times up to modernity, moving across the Mycenaean, Classical, Hellenistic, Roman, Byzantine, Venetian, and Ottoman periods. Also featuring a public library, this is Athens' largest museum. It was built between 1866 and 1889 to serve as a gathering place for a small part of the immense wealth of artifacts, tools, statues, gravestones, and other historical finds originating from the area of the world thought of as the cradle of Western civilization.

Just as at the Acropolis Museum, the visitor is guided through a thematic itinerary comprising five areas on two floors: prehistoric times, sculptures, ceramics, bronzes, and Egyptian collections.

Among the museum's most precious pieces is the Mask of Agamemnon, a gold foil funeral mask unearthed in 1876 in Mycenae by Heinrich Schliemann, the amateur archaeologist who had discovered the ruins of the ancient city of Troy in 1872, and the fabled Treasure of Priam in 1873. It is named after the legendary Achaean King Agamemnon, who, after gathering the Greek forces and organizing the fleet, waged war against Troy to retrieve Helen, likely a daughter of Zeus, who had been kidnapped by Paris, a Trojan prince and son of King Priam.

Another masterpiece not to miss is the bronze statue of Zeus, king of the gods (or possibly Poseidon, god of the sea), dating back to 460 BCE and considered one of the highest examples of Classical Greece's art that arrived intact to the present day. It was discovered in 1926 off the coast of Artemisium – hence its name Zeus of Artemisium – near the wreck of a Roman ship. The statue is slightly bigger-than-life size, and its vigorous body is a stunning paragon of perfect proportions. Its pose suggests that it depicts either Zeus hurling a bolt or Poseidon throwing his trident.

The museum's southern wing houses the Epigraphic Museum, founded in 1895, the most important of its kind in the world, holding more than 14,000 inscriptions from Ancient Greece.

* * *

Other notable museums include:

The Byzantine and Christian Museum, founded in 1914, showcases more than three thousand pieces, mostly from Athens' time as a part of the Byzantine Empire, including religious icons, manuscripts, embroideries, mosaics, sculptures, ceramics, and paintings.

The Museum of Cycladic Art, inaugurated in 1986, is housed in the Stathatos Mansion, a remarkable neoclassical townhouse by the Bavarian architect Ernst Ziller. It is home to one of the most extensive private collections of Cycladic art worldwide, featuring numerous examples of figurines, vases, tools, weapons, and pottery from Greece's Cycladic islands (Andros, Naxos, Antiparos, Amorgos, and Santorini) of the Early Bronze Age, but also from Cyprus and Ancient Greece.

The Benaki Museum of Greek Culture, inaugurated in 1930, is a popular private museum founded by the wealthy merchant and prominent art collector Antonis Benakis, who donated his impressive collection of 45,000 historical pieces gathered over thirty-five years as well as his beautiful neoclassical family mansion to create it. In the forty halls of the museum, pieces such as jewelry, wood carvings, Byzantine works, ceramics, Greek liturgical costumes, manuscripts, and religious icons are exhibited.

From the same author

Rome – Its History, Its Art, Its Landmarks

Venice – Its History, Its Art, Its Landmarks

Florence – Its History, Its Art, Its Landmarks

Italy's Finest – Rome, Venice, Florence (Omnibus edition)

Las Vegas The Grand – The Strip, the Casinos, the Mob, the Stars

Printed in Great Britain
by Amazon